FaithBuilders #4—
How to Eat an Orange

FaithBuilders #4—
How to Eat an Orange

. . . and More Lessons for Kids

Sheryl Bruinsma

Baker Books

A Division of Baker Book House Co
Grand Rapids, Michigan 49516

© 1991 by Sheryl Bruinsma

Published by Baker Books
a division of Baker Book House Company
P.O. Box 6287, Grand Rapids, MI 49516-6287

New paperback edition published 2001

Previously published under the title *Object Lessons for Every Occasion*

Printed in the United States of America

ISBN 0-8010-6348-5

For current information about all releases from Baker Book House, visit our web site:
                    http://www.bakerbooks.com

to
Uncle John Smilde
and his more than 80 years
of loving and distributing books

Contents

Lessons for Elementary School Students

Lessons for Older Students

List of Scripture References

Genesis
1:31a—42

1 Kings
19:12—80

Psalms
19:12b—26
51:10—22
95:2—16

Proverbs
23:7b—48

Ecclesiastes
3:1–2—36

Matthew
1:21—18
2:1–2—24
5:4—86
5:12a—52
5:16—64
6:24—82
6:26—70

Luke
2:19—20

John
3:16—40
10:10b—28

Acts
1:8—72

2:1–4—30
17:11b—62

Romans
12:9b—38

1 Corinthians
15:33—56
15:34a—68

Galatians
5:22–23a—30

Ephesians
3:17a—54
5:19—60

Philippians
4:13—34

Colossians
3:23—14

Hebrews
10:17—66
11:1—76

James
2:18—84

2 Peter
1:7—46
3:18—78

1 John
4:19—50

Using This Book

Jesus often used parables to clarify his teachings to his followers. Parables, analogies, or object lessons are still important tools in Christian education. They help clarify difficult concepts and make them more meaningful as well as hold the attention of the children. The purpose of this book is to provide ministers, teachers, and parents with easily obtainable objects and workable comparisons to important Christian truths.

Each lesson begins with an outline to summarize the basic idea. This outline will also assist the speaker in remembering effective introductory and closing remarks. Lessons are given on three levels, with concepts and vocabulary appropriate to each level: very young children (the key to speaking to young ones is to keep it simple and repetitious); elementary-aged children, and older students. The presenter is, of course, the best judge of the needs and abilities of the children who are receiving the lesson. Be enthusiastic when presenting a lesson, for this generates in the children a sense of the excitement of God's wonderful messages to them.

The lessons in this book are also useful for family devotions. The texts can be read by the children or the parents. Together they can grow spiritually in a unique and meaningful way.

Special Days

1

We Are a Team
New Season

Object: A bowling ball

Lesson: It takes everyone's accepting his or her responsibilities, doing his or her best, and working together to accomplish Christian group goals.

Text: Whatever you do, work at it with all your heart, as though you were working for God and not for men (Col. 3:23).

Outline

Introduce object: How many of you have ever gone bowling?

1. You need to take turns.
2. Lift the heavy ball (do the difficult task).
3. Aim straight (for the glory of God).
4. While everyone is important, it is the team score that really counts.

Conclusion: Adding up what everyone has done makes us a team!

How many of you have ever gone bowling? I brought a bowling ball with me today because it can help me tell you important things about beginning our new season.

When you go bowling, you have to take turns. This is easy to understand because the point of bowling is to roll this heavy ball down the middle of the bowling alley and knock over as many pins as you can. If two or more people tried to throw the ball at once, they would bang into each other, the balls would bang into each other, and nobody would know who had knocked down which pins. In our new season, we should remember to take turns and to be kind to others.

This ball is really heavy, but to play the game I have to pick it up and throw it down the alley. Sometimes you will be asked to do a task that might seem difficult, but if you are going to be a good team member, you will have to try to do it. We want to do our best for God, and he will help us!

When you throw the ball, you need to aim straight. If your ball goes off to the side, it will fall into the gutter and it won't be able to hit any pins. So also we want to aim everything we do straight for the glory of God. With this as our goal, how can we go wrong!

We are doing team bowling. Everybody's score is important, but what really counts is the total score. Adding up what everyone has done makes us a team!

Thankful for Many Things

Thanksgiving

Object: A bag containing small objects such as soap, pen, pencil, small packet of tissues, and knife

Lesson: Using common, everyday objects, help the children discover many things for which to be thankful to God.

Text: Let us come before him [God] with thanksgiving (Ps. 95:2).

Outline

Introduce object: We should be thankful to God every day of our lives, but sometimes we forget.

1. Have the children name what they are thankful for.
2. Other things for which to be thankful are:
    a. soap—being able to be clean
    b. pen and pencil—being able to write ideas and messages
    c. small packet of tissues—the comfort and convenience of our world
    d. knife—being able to use small tools

Conclusion: Now that we have taken a look at some other suggestions for which to be thankful, can you think of more?

16

We should be thankful to God every day of our lives, but sometimes we forget. That is why we have Thanksgiving Day. On this day we make a special effort to think of all that God has given us and done for us. It is usually easy to remember the big ones. Tell me some of the things for which you want to thank God. Yes, there are our homes, parents, food and clothes, schools and teachers, friends, pets, and health—so many! These are all big and important. I hope you remember to thank God often for them. Do you?

In this bag I have a collection of objects which will help us think of other items for which we should be thankful. Here is a bar of soap. Even if you don't like to wash, think of what it would be like if you could never get really clean because you lived in a place where you did not have soap or water. I thank God that I can get clean!

Next I have a pen and pencil. There are so many ways we use pens or pencils to write out thoughts or messages. I thank God for ideas and words and the ability to write them down! In here I also have a small packet of tissues. Stop and think for a minute what it would be like if we did not have articles like tissues, toothbrushes, combs, and so forth. I thank God he has made the world a comfortable and convenient place to live.

There are many small tools I could have put in the bag—like scissors, fork, or screwdriver. I have a knife in here because I have been on picnics without one. I thank God for these and the ability to use them. Now that we have taken a look at some other things for which to be thankful, can you think of more?

Open Up

Advent

Object: A folded garland made of foil or tissue paper. This garland is a decoration that comes folded flat but extends several feet when opened up.

Lesson: Advent is a time to prepare your heart for Christmas.

Text: She will have a son, and you will name him Jesus—because he will save his people from their sins (Matt. 1:21).

Outline

Introduce object: This decoration I have in my hand is called a garland.

1. We decorate to get ready for Christmas. We get our hearts ready by thinking of the true meaning of Christmas.
2. This garland must be opened up to be enjoyed. We must open up to the joy of the season.

Conclusion: Let's hope that when you are fully opened up, you will not want to close again either.

This decoration I have in my hand is called a garland. It doesn't look like much now because it

18

comes folded flat. You have to stretch it out to be able to enjoy the colors and design.

This time of year is called Advent—the season in which we get ready for celebrating Jesus' birthday, or Christmas. We get our rooms ready by cleaning and decorating. I'm going to use this garland to hang over the archway between our living room and dining room. I'm getting this and other decorations ready now even though Christmas is still a few weeks away because it takes time to get ready properly.

We also need to get our hearts ready for Christmas. To do this, we think about the true meaning of Christmas and how wonderful it is that God sent his only Son to earth as a baby for us to love and worship. The baby Jesus will grow up and save his people from their sins. When we think of this it really becomes exciting to prepare for such a special event.

The garland is a truly unusual decoration because of the way it is made. When it is opened up, you can see how the paper is attached to make this interesting design. We also become more beautiful when we are opened up. Instead of being all tucked together, thinking only of ourselves and our problems or responsibilities, we need to open up to the joy and excitement of the season. Christmas is such a wonderful time that we want to enjoy all that God has to offer us.

Once this garland has been opened up, it is pretty hard to get it back into the package. Let's hope that when you are fully opened up, you will not want to close again either.

Don't Be a Tree

Christmas

> **Object:** Dress like a tree. Wear a sweater so that you can hook ornaments onto yourself. Drape a string of lights over your shoulders.
>
> **Lesson:** The true joy of Christmas is on the inside.
>
> **Text:** Mary remembered all these things and thought deeply about them (Luke 2:19).

Outline

Introduce object: I really dressed up for Christmas this year.

1. Wearing Christmas on the outside is limiting.
2. With Christmas on the inside, you can have the fullness of light, joy, hope, and peace, which can shine through you.

Conclusion: Don't be a tree; be a happy, celebrating, Christian person.

I really dressed up for Christmas this year. These are some of my favorite ornaments. Do you like them? Here, let me plug in my lights. Everyone is going to know that I celebrate Christmas!

Something is wrong here. I'm not very comfortable. I can't sit down and I can't move far from the electrical outlet or my lights will go out. There has to be a better way to celebrate Christmas.

Now, if I were to have the special ornaments and symbols of Christmas on the inside, I would certainly be able to get around better. I could have the light of Christ and the warm glow of God inside of me. I could also have the joy and hope and peace of this season inside where I can savor it all of the time. It will still shine through my face and everyone will be able to tell by the things I say and do that I love Jesus and look forward to celebrating his birthday!

This is such a wonderful time of the year. You don't have to wear Christmas decorations on the outside, but make sure you have the best of God's season on the inside! Don't be a tree; be a happy, celebrating, Christian *person*.

A New Book Bag

New Year

Object: A new or new-looking book bag (or a suitcase or backpack)

Lesson: A new year symbolizes a fresh start, a new chance to become a better Christian.

Text: Create a pure heart in me, O God, and put a new and loyal spirit in me (Ps. 51:10).

Outline

Introduce object: I love getting a new book bag.

1. Sort out the old, keeping the good.
2. Add what new things God would want of you.

Conclusion: What good things can you put into your new year?

I love getting a new book bag. It has no holes, no ink stains, no tattered edges, no tears from being dragged along the ground, and no sticky snack leftovers!

Into my new book bag I can put all of the books, pens, pencils, papers, and other things that I am going to need for school. Some of the items that I am already using are good, but there are others that I need to replace. I need more clean paper, a new book, and some sharpened pencils. This is like a new start—a new chance to be organized.

Today is the first day of a new year. In many ways having a new year is like having a new book bag. We can put the old things that are still good into our new year, add to them, and organize them so that our new year will be better. There were some things I did that God wanted me to do last year, like praying to him, going to church, trying to be kind and helpful. I will keep them.

Sometimes I was not as good as I wanted to be. I have made a "New Year's resolution," or promise, to be better. I am throwing away the bad thoughts and actions just like these old papers and worn-out pens and pencils. I will try to do something better in the new year. I want to spend more time helping people. I want to spend more time enjoying the wonderful world God gave us. There is room in my new year for all of the things I know God wants me to do. I need to stop and think for a while about the good, new actions I can take with the fresh, clean, wonderful new year that God has given me. What good deeds can you put into your new year?

Finding the King

Epiphany

Object: Anything being used to celebrate Epiphany or a Bible

Lesson: The wise men traveled far to find the king. Our spiritual journey is also long.

Text: Matthew 2:1–2.

Outline

Introduce object: This is the celebration of Epiphany—the time in which we remember the wise men who came from the East to find the baby Jesus.

1. Their trip was long—our spiritual journey is a lifetime of growth.
2. They needed directions—we have the Bible.
3. The road was dangerous—there are traps for Christians.
4. They needed food—we need spiritual food.
5. They had companionship—we have fellowship.

Conclusion: Yes, the trip is long and not always easy, but it certainly is worth it.

This is the celebration of Epiphany—the time in which we remember the wise men who came from the East to find the baby Jesus. We celebrate it separately from Christmas because it is believed the wise men didn't actually find the baby Jesus until he was about two years old. I like this celebration because there are so many things the wise men teach us.

We know that the wise men had a very long trip. Our spiritual journey is also a long one. Nobody is perfect overnight. We all need to strive to find the King and all that he has for us in our lives.

The wise men must have had some sort of map or set of directions. So too we have the Bible to guide us on our journey. I'm happy for these directions. It would be tough to find the King of kings without them. We would lose our way.

The wise men faced many dangers along the road. There were robbers and wild animals. The roads were bumpy and sometimes muddy. Christians face dangers along the road also. We can be robbed by pride and a wrong sense of self-worth. We can hit bumpy times or get stuck in a mud hole of sin.

I wonder what the wise men had to eat along the road. They certainly didn't have fast food or even fancy restaurants, but they had to eat! Christians need food also—spiritual food. They need to study, pray, meditate, and learn.

The wise men didn't travel alone. They had companionship. So, too, do Christians have companions. They have the fellowship of the other Christians who are also on their journey to find the King. Yes, the trip is long and not always easy, but it certainly is worth it.

7

Clean Between

Lent

Object: Dental floss

Lesson: Lent is a time of searching our hearts.

Text: Deliver me, LORD, from hidden faults! (Ps. 19:12b).

Outline

Introduce object: We all know you should brush your teeth regularly, but how many of you use dental floss?

1. You need to clean between your teeth to remove all food particles that cause decay.
2. To prepare for Lent, we need to search our hearts and minds.

Conclusion: When our hearts and minds are clean, we are ready to remember and appreciate what our wonderful Jesus did for us.

We all know you should brush your teeth regularly, but how many of you use dental floss? The toothbrush does a good job brushing the parts of our teeth that we can see, but it doesn't always get between the teeth where tiny bits of food can get stuck and cause tooth decay. Dental floss is designed to get between our teeth (*demonstrate*) and clean them completely. Yes, now my teeth are really clean.

This is the season of Lent. It is the time of year we prepare our hearts and minds for Jesus' death on the cross for our sins. Do you remember when we celebrated Advent—the time of preparation for Christmas? Lent is much like that. To prepare our hearts and minds we need to clean out bad thoughts and feelings—things that grow like tooth decay between our teeth. Sometimes, like tooth decay, we don't even know they are there. When we pray about it, God will show them to us and help us to clean them out. Then we need to shine up ourselves by thinking of the greatness of God's love and the amazing sacrifice of Jesus on the cross.

When our hearts and minds are clean, we are ready to remember and appreciate what our wonderful Jesus did for us.

New Life

Easter

Object: A branch with leaves beginning to grow

Lesson: Easter means new life, a time of dedication and renewal

Text: "I have come in order that you might have life—life in all its fullness" (John 10:10b).

Outline

Introduce object: The Easter season is a wonderful time of celebration.

1. New leaves begin to grow—Christians grow.
2. What if leaves refused to continue growing; what if Christians refuse to continue growing?
3. This new life happens every year—Christians need frequent renewal and dedication.

Conclusion: Thank you, Jesus, for dying for us. Thank you for giving us new life.

The Easter season is a wonderful time of celebration. In it we remember Jesus' dying on the cross and rising again. He gives us new life. This branch will help me explain new life. Take a close look at the new, little leaves beginning to form on this branch. Do you see each tiny leaf? It looks just like the big leaf it will become, but it is just beginning to grow.

Jesus' dying gives us new life. This is a season of renewing and rededicating ourselves to him. It is a time to grow. Like this tiny leaf, we see what we can be. We will grow and grow until we become the big, beautiful Christian God wants us to be.

What if this branch said: "I'm tired of doing this every year. I'm not going to grow this year. I'm just going to stay the way I am now." Think of how ugly this branch will look next to the other branches that have beautiful leaves growing on them. So, too, some people think that they do not need to grow anymore. They can stay just the way they are. Too bad for them!

The tree this branch comes from grows new leaves every year and has done this for its whole life. Christians need to renew themselves often as well. We need to remember what Jesus did for us and to thank him and promise to live for him. We need to rededicate ourselves to him.

Thank you, Jesus, for dying for us. Thank you for giving us new life.

A Full, Bubbly Life

Pentecost

Object: A bottle of soda (the larger, the better) and a large balloon. Blow up the balloon and let the air out first so it will expand more easily with the carbonation. During the lesson, open the soda bottle and place the balloon over the entire top of the bottle. Then shake the soda back and forth to release the carbonation. This causes the balloon to expand.

Lesson: The power of the Holy Spirit came to the believers on Pentecost and is still an important force.

Text: Acts 2:1–4; Galatians 5:22–23a.

Outline

Introduce object: (*Give meaning of Pentecost.*) Watch while I put this balloon on the top of the bottle and shake and pour the soda around.

1. Power—gas blows up the balloon; the Holy Spirit gives power to our Christian lives.
2. Bubbles—drinking soda is bubbly; the Holy Spirit gives us joy (a bubbly spirit).

Conclusion: Let the Holy Spirit produce in you love, joy, peace, patience, kindness, goodness, faithfulness, humility, and self-control.

Today we celebrate Pentecost—the coming of the Holy Spirit to the early church. It was a wonderful and exciting time for them. First they heard a sound like a strong wind blowing right in the house where they were. Then flames of fire touched each one of them, only they were not burned. Even more surprising, they each began to speak in a language they had not studied. People who knew this language could understand what they said. That must have been really exciting. The best part is that the Holy Spirit is still with us today.

You know that inside of this soda bottle is a gas that gives little bubbles when we drink it. We take that for granted, but watch while I put this balloon on the top of the bottle and shake the soda around. The balloon grows bigger and bigger. Did you have any idea how powerful the gas in this soda really is?

The Holy Spirit is a powerful force in and around us. He gives us the power to live complete and fulfilling Christian lives. He gives us the help and power to accomplish more for God than we ever thought possible.

Just as the carbonation in the bottle gives us a bubbly, tickling feeling, so too the Holy Spirit gives us the joyful feeling of a triumphant Christian life.

Thank God for the power and exciting force of the Holy Spirit in this world. Use this power for a more bubbly Christian life. Let the Holy Spirit produce in you love, joy, peace, patience, kindness, goodness, faithfulness, humility, and self-control.

Current Issues

10

It's Not Your Fault

Divorce

Object: An apple that has been cut in half and pressed back together.

Lesson: Helping children cope with divorce.

Text: I have the strength to face all conditions by the power that Christ gives me (Phil. 4:13).

Outline

Introduce object: This looks like a delicious, whole, ripe apple.

1. The apple is cut. Because some of your parents are not together, the family (like this apple) is not whole.
2. You did not cut the apple—you are not at fault for the divorce.
3. You cannot fix the apple—you cannot fix the divorce.
4. Nothing else is cut—you are not divorced.

Conclusion: The people in the Bible faced hard times but God gave them the strength to get through them. He will do this for you too.

This looks like a delicious, whole, ripe apple. I brought it with me today to help explain something important—divorce.

34

Look, actually this apple is cut in half. We weren't expecting that. It doesn't look right. That's what happens when parents get divorced—we weren't expecting it and it doesn't look right.

Did you cut the apple? No, you did not do it. It is not your fault. When your parents get divorced, you are not to blame either. You did not do it, and it is not your fault. Ask God to help you not to feel that way.

Can you put this apple back together again? No, you can't. Neither can you put your parents back together again. You did not break them apart and you cannot fix them again. Ask God to help you accept what you cannot change.

Is anything but this apple cut? No, there is nothing else cut. When parents divorce each other, they do not divorce the children. They still love you just as much as they did before. Sometimes they try to show their love by buying too many things for you. You will have to help them understand that you still love them, and they don't have to do this. Sometimes they fight and you get caught in the middle. You will have to ask God to give you the strength and wisdom to stay out of their disagreements. Divorce is difficult, but God can help by giving you the strength you need to go on with your life and make the best of it. The people in the Bible faced hard times, but God gave them the strength to get through them. He will do this for you too.

11

A Time to Live, A Time to Die

Death

Object: A picture of a pet that has died.

Lesson: Death is a natural part of living.

Text: To every thing there is a season, and a time to every purpose under the heaven: A time to be born, and a time to die; a time to plant, and a time to pluck up that which is planted (Eccles. 3:1–2 KJV).

Outline

Introduce object: How many of you have pets?

1. Everything that lives eventually dies.
2. When someone we love dies, we grieve.
3. Memories comfort us.
4. People are special because they have souls that live on.

Conclusion: Loving, dying, and grieving are all an important part of living.

How many of you have pets? Pets are wonderful. We play with them, take care of them, and love them. Best of all, they accept us completely for what we are.

The sad part about having pets is that they eventually die. Death is sad but it is natural. Everything in nature eventually dies. The flowers die. Animals die. People die. The Bible tells us that everybody has a time to be born and a time to die. We know this and accept it as God's plan.

When my pet died, I cried. The whole family cried. Being sad and even angry is part of what we call grief. We need to grieve when someone we love dies. So we cry and are sad and lonely without them. It is natural for us to have tears in our eyes and lumps in our throats.

I have a picture of my pet and I will never forget her. Our memories of those we love stay with us even after they are gone. We are sad when they leave but they are never completely gone because we keep a part of them in our hearts and our memories. This helps us feel better.

When people we love die, we have the same kinds of feelings of loss and loneliness and hurt as we do for our loved pets, except that the feelings are usually stronger.

People are special because they have a soul—the part of them that loves God. This soul does not die but follows the light of Jesus into the place he has prepared for them. We miss those who die, but a bit of us has to be happy for them because they have gone to a wonderful place.

Loving, dying, and grieving are all an important part of living.

12

You Don't Have to Play

Drugs

Object: A pillow

Lesson: Don't do drugs.

Text: Hate what is evil, hold on to what is good (Rom. 12:9b).

Outline

Introduce object: Let's pretend that I have a new game to play today that is very dangerous.

1. Just because others are doing it, you don't have to play.
2. Just because a person you like or trust tells you to, you don't have to join.
3. Even when drugs are forced on you, you can resist.

Conclusion: You don't have to play.

Let's pretend that I have a new game to play today that is very dangerous. You have to imagine that inside of this pillow is a bomb. When you catch it, it will explode. How many of you would like to play? I'm using this game to help me talk about drugs. Drugs are pills and other dangerous medicines. If you would not like to play this new, dangerous game, you don't have to play! Nobody can force you to play. Just remember that if you get into a situation where there is pressure, you do not have to do it. If you know what others are doing is wrong, don't do it.

Some of you thought that if *I* suggested the game, it might be okay to try. That is the hard part about drugs. Sometimes a person you like or trust tells you to try. If this pillow were really going to explode in your hands, would you still want to play? Think about it. Don't just do it because I tell you to.

Suppose I throw this pillow at you. Will you catch it? It will be hard to step aside or even let it hit you, but as long as you don't catch it, it won't explode. Some of you might have drugs thrown at you, forced in your face, shoved in your hand. Sometimes people tease you or pester you to try them. It's going to be hard to refuse. Would you catch the pillow if you knew it would explode?

Some people live in a land of exploding pillows. Many people around them are using drugs and it is very hard for them to avoid them. Thank God that is not you.

We are only pretending that this pillow will explode. We *know* that using drugs will blow up the person's self-confidence, honesty, integrity. You don't have to play.

13

All Apples Have Stars Inside

Prejudice

Object: A red, a yellow, and a green apple (two of the three would work) and a knife. (*Note: When you cut the apple, slice around the middle, not from stem to blossom end, to show the star shape in the core*).

Lesson: Prejudice is against God's desire for his people.

Text: For God loved the world so much that he gave his only Son, so that everyone who believes in him may not die but have eternal life (John 3:16).

Outline

Introduce object: There is nothing like a nice juicy apple.

1. All colors of apples are the same inside and so are people.
2. All apples have a star inside and people that love God have his love inside.

Conclusion: You can tell them that God doesn't care about their color and neither do you.

There is nothing like a nice juicy apple. I have with me a red one, a yellow one, and a green one.

They are all ripe and ready to eat. Which one should I choose? Which one looks best to you?

Let's see, the red apple must be red inside, right? No? You've eaten a red apple before and it was white inside? Well, then, this yellow apple, is it yellow inside? No? Then surely this green apple must be green inside. Do you think I'm being silly to say that? We all know that apples are white inside. We know what to expect when we bite into an apple.

People come in different colors too. It is just as silly to think that a black person is black inside or an Oriental person that we call yellow is yellow inside. *Prejudice* means that you expect people to act or think a certain way because of the way they look. We usually get this from other people telling us. Would you believe a person who told you that a ripe, green apple was green inside? You can look for yourself!

God looks at the inside of a person. Let's cut open these apples and look at the inside. Yes, the insides are all white. What a pity it would have been if we didn't want one of these delicious apples because of that we thought was inside. Oh, look! Each of these apples has a star inside. That reminds me that each of God's children has within himself or herself the love of God—whatever the color on the outside. I hope that nobody ever tries to tell you that certain people are not good because of their color on the outside. You can tell them that God doesn't care about a person's color and neither do you!

14

Keep Your Earth Clean

Pollution

Object: A bag of trash.

Lesson: God gave us this world, and we are responsible for it.

Text: God looked at everything he had made, and he was very pleased (Gen. 1:31a).

Outline

Introduce object: This is a bag of trash.

1. Don't litter or pollute.
2. Clean up, recycle, don't buy plastic bags or styrofoam.
3. Conserve energy.

Conclusion: This is how we use God's world responsibly.

This is a bag of trash. Nobody likes trash. Why would I want to bring a bag of it in here! Listen and it will help me tell you about something very important.

God gave us this earth clean and beautiful. The Indians knew this and they treated the earth like a person. Would you throw trash on a person? They would not litter or pollute the earth or harm it in any way.

Then along came the white people. We cut down the trees, dug big holes in the earth, dumped poison in the rivers, released harmful chemicals into the air, and threw trash on the ground.

Now it is up to you and me to make up for that. If I dropped one of these pieces of paper on the floor and walked away, would you pick it up or would you just say that you did not drop it so you don't have to pick it up? What do you think God would like you to do? If you see a mess, clean it up.

Many cities now have recycling programs. Instead of throwing all of our trash together, we can put all cans, all glass, all newspapers, and so forth, in separate containers. This way we can use them again. God smiles at that.

Some plastic and styrofoam will stay on the earth forever. We have to bury it to get rid of it. Don't buy it or use it. God gave us many natural materials to use.

How would you feel if we ran out of clean water, heat for our houses, or electricity? You can help by not using too much. Turn off the lights and TV when you are not using them. Don't run the water unless you must have some and take only what you need. Put on a sweater instead of turning up the heat. This is how we use God's world responsibly.

Lessons for Very Young Children

15

Christian Character

Kinds of People

Object: Three bottles or jars of liquid: one with water and white vinegar, one with water and bleach, one with water and sugar

Lesson: God wants us to be kind, loving, gentle, helpful, and patient.

Text: To your godliness add brotherly affection; and to your brotherly affection add love (2 Peter 1:7).

Outline

Introduce object: I have three bottles of clear liquid with me today.

1. Vinegar and water—a sour, selfish, whining person
2. Bleach and water—a mean, unkind, dangerous person
3. Sugar and water—a kind, gentle, helpful, loving, patient person

Conclusion: Which kind of person are you?

I have three bottles of clear liquid with me today. The three bottles look alike. It is hard to tell there is any difference. When I smell what is in

46

them and then taste them, I can tell that they are very different. You should never taste anything if you don't know what it is, but I put the liquids into the bottles, so I know what they are.

This first bottle smells and tastes sour. It is vinegar and water. If this were a person, I would say that he or she is sour, sad, whining, selfish, unhappy. Does this sound like the kind of person you would like to be? No, this is not the kind of person God wants you to be either.

The next bottle smells like a swimming pool. It is bleach and water. Bleach is poison so I know better than to drink what is in this bottle. Would you like a nice big mouthful of swimming pool water? If this were a person, I would say that he or she is dangerous. A person like this might do bad things to you or try to get you to do bad things. Mean people might try to bully you or hit or tease you. They are unkind to people and others do not like them. Would you like to be like this person?

The last bottle smells sweet. I can taste it because I know it is sugar water. If this were a person, he or she would be kind and helpful. This person would smile at people and be patient with them. This person would take turns and be gentle. This person would love God and show God's love to other people. Which kind of person are you?

16

You Are Not Sound-Activated

Special Abilities

Object: A sound-activated toy (doll, stuffed animal, dancing flower).

Lesson: God has given you a heart to love and a mind to think.

Text: What he thinks is what he really is (Prov. 23:7b).

Outline

Introduce object: This is a new kind of doll.

1. The doll works by outside noises and makes only certain moves.
2. You work from the inside. God has given you a heart to love and a mind to listen, think, and decide.
3. Give situations where children have to think and respond.

Conclusion: Thank God for making you special.

This is a new kind of doll. When you make a noise, it starts to move. Watch it while I clap my hands. Now you say something to it and it will move. It almost looks like this is a real, live baby.

This doll has batteries inside of it that are turned on by sound. When the sounds stop, the doll stops. When the doll is alone in a quiet room, it can't move. It has no mind of its own. If you turn it off or take the batteries out, it won't work at all.

You can move your arms and legs like this doll. You can move your mouth like this doll. But you don't have to have *noise* to make you move. You work from the *inside*. God has given you a mind to think about what you want to do. He has given you a heart to love. He has given you the ability to decide if something is good to do. He has given you ears to listen to what your parents and teachers tell you to do. He has given you the ability to decide if what other children tell you to do is right or wrong.

This doll can only move a few ways. It will never be able to think of any new moves. It will never be able to decide which way it wants to move. Aren't you glad you can? Since God has given you this special power, let's see if you can say *yes* or *no* to these questions. When your ball rolls out into a busy street, are you going to run out into the street after it? If you see someone sad or lonely, will you give them a hug? When you don't get your own way, will you kick and scream? When your mother tells you to pick up your toys, will you do it? If your friend tells you to lie, will you do it? Thank God for making you special.

17

More Powerful Than a Pinwheel

God's Love

Object: A handmade pinwheel. Take a square piece of paper (construction paper thickness is better but regular paper will do). Draw a line from corner to opposite corner forming a large *X*. Cut from each corner halfway to the center. Fold down each point *X* over the center point, hold. Push a straight pin through the five thicknesses of paper into the side of a pencil eraser.

Lesson: God's love is a powerful force in our lives.

Text: We love because God first loved us (1 John 4:19).

Outline

Introduce object: How many of you have ever made your own pinwheel? Let me show you how (*demonstrate*).

1. You can't see the air or God's love, but you can see what it does.
2. The air and God's love are all around us and in us.
3. The air is powerful; God's love is more powerful.

Conclusion: Even more important than that is the truth that God loves me and he loves you, and you, and you (*point to each child or call him or her by name*).

How many of you have ever made your own pinwheel? Let me show you how. (*Demonstrate*.)

What makes the pinwheel go around is the air. You can't see the air but you can see it move the pinwheel. The love of God is much like that. You can't see it, but you certainly can see what it can do. The love of God can make people love each other. It can make you feel warm and happy, knowing that God loves you. It can give you the strength to do something that you need to do.

The air that moves this pinwheel is all around us. I can breathe the air in and blow it out and make the pinwheel move, or I can move the pinwheel through the air and it turns. God's love is all around us. We can see it in the wonderful world he gave us. We can see it in the people he loves and who love him. We can breathe it in and "blow it out" by loving others around us.

When you think of it, the air is powerful. When I move this pinwheel through the still, invisible air, the pinwheel moves. It's almost like magic. Well, we know the love of God is powerful. It can even make people who are fighting stop and love each other. That's better than magic.

God's love is better than the air because it is more powerful. Even more important than that is the truth that God loves me and he loves you, and you, and you (*point to each child or call him or her by name*).

18

In Secret

Helping Others

Object: A helium-filled balloon (It does not have to be fresh.)

Lesson: Do good deeds in secret and let people wonder who did them.

Text: Be happy and glad, for a great reward is kept for you in heaven (Matt. 5:12a).

Outline

Introduce object: We bought helium balloons at a fair.

1. The balloons that get away come down and somebody wonders where they came from.
2. Do good deeds and let someone wonder who did them.

Conclusion: Let's think of some nice, *secret* things we can do.

We bought helium balloons at a fair. Like this one, the balloons wanted to float away into the sky. Did you ever see a helium balloon that got away? It floats up, up, up, and out of sight. During a parade you can usually see several balloons dancing around the buildings and heading for open sky.

Have you ever wondered where the balloons go? Eventually the helium escapes through the too-small-to-see holes in the balloon and the balloon begins to come down. Sometimes children catch them and take them home.

A helium balloon floated into our yard recently. I wondered where it had come from and who had lost it. Sometimes people attach messages to helium balloons and let them go on purpose, but there was no message.

As I stood there thinking about the balloon and where it had come from, something the Bible tells us began to take on new meaning. I knew that God tells us to do nice things for people without telling them—this makes our reward in heaven greater. I realized that there is something else that makes doing secret good deeds special. The person wonders and wonders who did the good deed and where the special favor came from. I like the thought of giving a gift to someone and having them say, "I wonder where this came from. Who would do such a nice thing?" Or I could do something for somebody without them seeing me and have them say, "Now who could have done this? I wonder!"

Doesn't this sound like fun to do? Let's think of some nice, secret things we can do.

19

It Rattles

Christ on the Inside

Object: A baby rattle (and/or a container with rice or dried beans inside)

Lesson: Christians have Christ in their hearts.

Text: And pray that Christ will make his home in our hearts through faith (Eph. 3:17a).

Outline

Introduce object: One of the first toys we give a baby is a rattle.

1. It is not a rattle just because it is with the other rattles (not a Christian because the person is with other Christians).
2. It is not a rattle when something is taped to the outside (not a Christian just because he or she tries to look like one on outside).
3. What rattles is on the inside (Christians have Christ in their hearts).

Conclusion: Does Christ live inside of you?

One of the first toys we give a baby is a rattle. People have been doing it for years. Before they had plastic rattles like this one, people put rice or dried beans in a can or box and shook it. The noise of the rattle gets the baby's attention and he stops crying. When they get a little older, babies like to pick up the rattles and make the noise themselves.

A rattle is called a *rattle* because it has something inside that rattles. It doesn't become a rattle just because it is kept with other rattles. Christians are special people, but they don't become Christians by being with other Christians. Just sitting in church doesn't make a person a Christian any more than sitting with the rattles makes a toy a rattle.

I could not make a rattle by taping some little pieces on the outside of this toy. It still wouldn't rattle. So, too, trying to look like a Christian on the outside doesn't make a person a Christian. The Bible warns about people who make big speeches and tell everyone how great they are but are empty on the inside.

Yes, a rattle is a rattle because it has something inside that rattles. A Christian is a Christian because he or she loves Christ inside. When Christ lives inside, the person has a special way of believing, thinking, feeling, and living. Christ is at the very center of the person. Does Christ live inside of you?

Good Companions

Contagions, Good and Bad

Object: Choose a child who has a nice smile to help you.

Lesson: Choose good companions.

Text: Do not be fooled, "Bad companions ruin good character" (1 Cor. 15:33).

Outline

Introduce object: I need someone who has a nice big smile to help me.

1. Some of what we catch from people are okay—smiles, yawns.
2. Some we try to avoid—colds, measles, chicken pox, mumps.
3. Bad companions, those who lie, steal, cheat, or are rude, we must avoid completely.

Conclusion: Now, would you rather catch this sweet smile of [name] or would you like to walk around with an unpleasant attitude like the one you can see on my face now (*look grumpy*)?

I need someone who has a nice big smile to help me. [Name,] that is a beautiful smile. Come up here and show everyone. Now look at everyone smile back at you. You see, a smile is catching. That is why we say, "If you see someone without a smile, give them one of yours." Something else that is catching is a yawn. Let's see if we can get someone else to yawn by giving a big yawn in front of them.

Smiles are good to catch. We like to be around happy people. God likes us to be cheerful Christians.

Colds, measles, chicken pox, and mumps are also catching. Some people have bad habits or are unpleasant. We don't want to get too close to these. I wouldn't want to catch a frown or a bad habit.

There are other people that should be avoided completely. We can also "catch" things from hanging around with people who lie, cheat, steal, or are rude. The Bible warns us about having bad companions. We become like the people we are with. We may go with them to places where we should not go. We may begin to use words that God and our parents do not want us to use. We may begin to tell lies or cheat in school—actions we would not have otherwise have taken.

Be careful about your choice of friends. You become like the people you are with for long periods of time. Now, would you rather catch this sweet smile of [name's] or would you like to walk around with an unpleasant attitude like the one you can see on my face now?

Lessons
for Elementary
School Students

21

A Singing Balloon

Singing for God

Object: A balloon.

Lesson: Sing to the glory of God with your heart and mind.

Text: Speak to one another with the words of psalms, hymns, and sacred songs; sing hymns and psalms to the Lord with praise in your hearts (Eph. 5:19).

Outline

Introduce object: Did you ever hear a balloon sing?

1. Our physical structure is similar to the balloon.
2. We have the God-given ability to make happy sounds on pitch.
3. True singing is meaning the words. We can sing to glorify God.

Conclusion: Just remember, without using your heart and mind, you might as well be a balloon.

Did you ever hear a balloon sing? Listen while this balloon sings for you. (*Demonstrate:* Blow up the balloon. Using both hands, pinch the mouth of the balloon. As you allow air to escape, stretch the mouth of the balloon so that the sound changes pitch.)

When we sing, our voices work similarly to the way this balloon sings. First we need to take a deep breath, just as I blew up the balloon. Then the air rushes past our vocal cords and makes them vibrate, just as the air made the two sides of the mouth of the balloon vibrate. Our vocal cords stretch to change the sound to a higher pitch, just as the balloon's sound became higher when I stretched the mouth of the balloon.

We usually sound better than a balloon when we sing because God has given us such wonderful equipment. We can hum on pitch or sing songs that we have heard. When we sing any old song without thinking, we are just making happy sounds. That's still not true singing.

The big difference with people is that we can sing words that we mean, and then our singing carries a message. The song "Jesus Loves Me" has a powerful message. Can you think of other songs that we sing that have a meaningful message? God wants us to sing songs about him and to *mean* what we sing. People can also write songs and words for songs. What a wonderful way to praise God and to let everyone around us know how we feel.

This poor balloon doesn't know what it is missing. Just remember, without using your heart and mind, you might as well be a balloon.

Read It

God's Word

> **Object:** A box of candy (cookies could be substituted)
>
> **Lesson:** The Bible needs to be read.
>
> **Text:** They listened to the message with great eagerness, and every day they studied the Scriptures (Acts 17:11b).

Outline

Introduce object: This is a box of delicious-looking candy.

1. Candy—you don't put it on the table and leave it opened and untouched, but you eat it.
2. Bible—you don't put it on a table and leave it opened and unread, but you read and study it.

Conclusion: Is there anyone here who does not know what to do with a Bible?

This is a box of delicious-looking candy. I wonder what I should do with it.

I've never had this kind of candy before. Maybe I should take it home and put it on the shelf. No, it should be where I can see it. I'll put it on the end table. Does that sound like what I should do with it? No? You say I should open it? All right, I'll take this paper off and open the box. Yes, this does look like good candy. I'll leave the open box right here where everyone can look at it and see how good it is. Don't you think it looks good? It smells good too! You still don't look happy. What else do you want me to do with it? Oh, you want to *eat* it! Silly me, why didn't I think of *eating* the candy.

That was not a very smart thing for me to do, but do you know what is even less smart? Some people take a Bible and put it on a shelf or on the end table. They know the Bible is good so they put it where everyone can see it. Some do even more than that. They open the Bible but they do not read it. In order to get the spiritual food, you need to *read* the Bible. Even better than just reading is studying the Bible.

Is there anyone here who does not know what to do with a Bible?

Suncatchers

Catching God's Love

> **Object:** A suncatcher—glass or plastic ornament designed to be hung in a window or in front of a light (can also use a piece of crystal)
>
> **Lesson:** Let God's light shine through you.
>
> **Text:** In the same way your light must shine before people, so that they will see the good things you do and praise your Father in heaven (Matt. 5:16).

Outline

Introduce object: How many of you have seen a suncatcher like this one hanging at a window?

1. It needs the light of the *sun* to show its design.
2. We need to show the light of the *Son*.
3. God has chosen *us* to show his light.

Conclusion: What is that I see shining through your face? Is it the love of God?

How many of you have seen a suncatcher like this one hanging at a window? Did you ever take one and put it in front of a dark cloth or object?

When you do this, you can hardly see the design. It certainly doesn't look like much, does it? A sun-catcher is meant to use the light of the sun to show its beautiful design.

People are like that too. They are meant to show the light of the *Son*: *s-o-n*; Jesus, God's Son. When you have this light inside of you, you glow with the love of God. Your faith shines out through your face and in your actions so that others can see. When you love God, you want to help people. When you love God, you want to be kind and generous. When you love God, you can ask him for patience. When your faith is shiny, people notice you are reflecting the light.

It is really quite remarkable that God has chosen us to shine his light. He could have picked something more reliable. People sometimes get gloomy and forget about their wonderful job. We certainly don't want to do that.

What is that I see shining through your face? Is it the love of God?

Forgive and Forget

Doing It God's Way

Object: Pressure paper, on which everything printed on the top copy appears on the bottom copy (carbon paper may also be used, or the back of the top paper may be covered in pencil lead).

Lesson: If we do not forgive and forget, we harm only ourselves.

Text: And then he says, "I will not remember their sins and evil deeds any longer" (Heb. 10:17).

Outline

Introduce object: This pressure paper reminds me of what happens to us when someone does something that hurts us or makes us angry.

1. When someone says they are sorry, we forgive them.
2. We need to forgive and forget, even when they have not said they are sorry—or we only harm ourselves.

Conclusion: God forgives and forgets the wrong things you do. He knows you need to do this also.

I'm going to write a note on this piece of paper. Look, the same message is on the second sheet. This is special pressure [or carbon] paper. Whatever is written on the top paper also appears on the bottom paper.

This pressure paper reminds me of what happens to us when someone does something that hurts us or makes us angry. If the person says that they are sorry, we tell them that we forgive them. We erase the top copy.

But is it always completely forgiven? Let's say that somebody took one of your toys and broke it. He (or she) said that he was sorry. You forgave that person but you did not ever really forgive and forget. Every time you saw that person, you remembered what he or she did. Every time you thought of your toy, you remembered what that person did. Now who is the person that is suffering? The person who took your toy thinks the whole thing is over. *You* are the one who is still bothered. Like this pressure paper, there is still a copy of the message underneath—you are still remembering inside. In your heart you have not truly forgiven and forgotten, and it will continue to bother you until you can manage to do this. It is even harder when the person does not say he/she is sorry. You may get more and more angry until you finally do something back. You may take it out on other people or on other toys. You are hurting *yourself*. You need to find a way to erase the message from both copies. If that can't be done, you need to tear up the bad copies and start again. God forgives and forgets the wrongs that you do. He knows you need to do this also.

Oct 28 2003

25

Rake Off the Dead Leaves

Renewal

Object: A bunch of dead, curled, dry leaves

Lesson: Get rid of inappropriate characteristics that interfere with the Christian life.

Text: Come back to your right senses and stop your sinful ways (1 Cor. 15:34a).

Outline

Introduce object: I don't usually bring a bunch of dead, dry leaves inside, but today they are going to help me tell you something.

1. When dead leaves lie on the grass, they need to be raked off.
2. For us to grow in our Christian lives we need to rake off things like selfishness, whining, self-pity, rudeness, fighting, and laziness.

Conclusion: Yes, it can be a lot of work, but it is rewarding to be free and clean and ready to grow again.

I don't usually bring a bunch of dead leaves inside, but today they are going to help me tell you something. The fall leaves are beautiful when they are on the trees. I enjoy the colors. The fall leaves are fun when they drift to the ground. I like to walk through them. Then the leaves lie there and turn brown and curl up. They are dead and useless. We need to rake them off the lawn because they are not good for the grass.

Sometimes we have dead, useless "leaves" on us—these get in the way of our living the life God wants us to lead. Characteristics like selfishness, whining, feeling sorry for ourselves, being rude or thoughtless, fighting with our brothers or sisters, or laziness. Do these sound like dead, dry leaves to you?

We certainly want to rake off and get rid of thoughts or actions like this. It can be a lot of work raking the leaves off the yard. Sometimes it takes a lot of effort to clean up our lives. We need to ask God to take each of these characteristics away. Then we need to make sure that it doesn't sneak back! I hate it when the leaves blow back on the lawn and I have to rake them off again!

Yes, it can be a lot of work, but it is rewarding to be free and clean and ready to grow again!

One Day at a Time

Trusting God

Object: A blanket (any article) being knitted or crocheted (or any craft item that must be constructed one step at a time)

Lesson: Trust God and live life one day at a time.

Text: Look at the birds flying around: they do not plant seeds, gather a harvest and put it in barns; yet your Father in heaven takes care of them! Aren't you worth much more than birds? (Matt. 6:26).

Outline

Introduce object: I am making this baby blanket.

1. It must be done one stitch at a time.
2. Live life one day at a time. Yesterday is over; God will take care of tomorrow.
3. Use today. Be responsible, enjoy God's world, be kind, trust God.

Conclusion: Live life one day at a time and thank God for it.

I am making this baby blanket. It is pink and blue because the baby isn't born yet, and I don't know if it will be a boy or a girl. First I make a row of pink and then I make a row of blue. I could make this any color I wanted but I have to do one row at a time. In fact, I have to do one stitch at a time. If I did a stitch here and a stitch there, they wouldn't stick together. Imagine trying to wrap a baby in a bunch of separate stitches! I can't do all of the pink stitches first and then all of the blue either or I wouldn't have this pattern.

God wants us to live our lives one day at a time, just like the blanket must be done one stitch at a time. He tells us not to worry about yesterday because that is over. He also tells us not to worry about the tomorrows because he will take care of them. Are you worried about going somewhere tomorrow? Trust God; he will take care of you. He takes care of the little birds and flowers; he will certainly take care of you. Some people spend all of today worrying about what will happen tomorrow, and when tomorrow gets here nothing happens. They wasted all of today worrying. Some people think, "I won't do that today. I can do it tomorrow." If they say that every day, it doesn't get done.

You have today: a day to do your chores and be good; a day to have fun and enjoy God's world; a day to show God's love in you by being kind to another person; and a day to trust God to give you what you need.

Live life one day at a time and thank God for it.

27

Let Your Light Shine

Witnessing

Object: Five candles, one with the wick snipped off at or below the wax; one with the wax whittled down so that the wick is too long; one with the wick snipped at about an eighth of an inch (too short); one with the wax whittled down so the wick is very long and bent over and pushed back into the candle (into a hole made with a hot needle or pin); and one candle with normal wick.

Lesson: Witness with a clear and simple message.

Text: But when the Holy Spirit comes upon you, you will be filled with power, and you will be witnesses for me in Jerusalem, in all of Judea and Samaria, and to the ends of the earth (Acts 1:8).

Outline

Introduce object: Candles give off a soft and inviting glow.

1. No wick—no message.
2. Wick too long—too much to say.
3. Wick too short—too little to say.
4. Wick looped—message sputtering.

5. Wick normal—clear, simple message.

Conclusion: Letting your light shine should not be difficult.

Candles give off a soft and inviting glow. Look at the ones I brought with me today. I would light this one for you but it has no wick. It has no way to let its light shine. If we think of this candle as a person, we could say that this person has no message. A candle with no wick is just a lump of wax.

This candle has a nice long wick. I'll light it for you. Look at that big flame. I'm afraid something might catch on fire. If this candle were a person, we might say that it blabs too much. Sometimes people talk so much that you really can't hear what they are trying to say. This candle won't do either.

I have another candle here with a very short wick. I seem to be having trouble lighting it. The flame won't catch well. When it does, it goes right out again. If this were a person, it wouldn't have enough to say.

My next candle has an interesting wick. It looks looped. What do you suppose will happen when I light it? Watch out, it is burning fiercely and quickly. Some people sputter and strain, trying so hard to give a message that should be clear and simple.

Finally this last candle has a wick that looks just right. It burns well also. If this were a person, it would have the love of God deep inside and be able to witness to this love in a simple and effective way. Letting your light shine should not be difficult.

Lessons for Older Students

Faith Works

Belief

> **Object:** A toaster (you could have toast in the toaster labeled: PEACE, JOY, and GOOD WORKS)
>
> **Lesson:** Faith is believing and trusting in the power of God in our lives.
>
> **Text:** To have faith is to be sure of the things we hope for, to be certain of the things we cannot see (Heb. 11:1).

Outline

Introduce object: It's this toaster's job to help me tell you about faith.

1. You don't have to know exactly how the toaster works to know that it *does* work.
2. You know it is working when you feel its warmth.
3. It needs to be cleaned to work properly.
4. You know it is a toaster if it makes toast (faith produces works).

Conclusion: Faith is believing in God completely.

It's this toaster's job to help me tell you about faith. Faith is believing in the power of God, knowing that God is real, and letting that make a difference in our lives.

I don't really understand exactly how this toaster works but I know that it does, just as I know that God is real and that his power works. You don't have to completely understand it to believe in it.

There are signs that this toaster is working. I can feel it getting warm. I can look inside and see the glow. I know that my faith is working when I feel the warmth inside of me that comes from God.

This toaster needs to be cleaned regularly to work right. You open this trap door in the bottom and clean out the crumbs. We also clean our hearts and minds of bad thoughts that keep our faith from working right.

The final proof that this toaster is working is that it makes toast. The final proof that our faith is working is that it produces love, joy, hope, and peace in our lives. Our faith also produces good works. We want to do nice things for others because our faith in God is strong and well. You know a toaster is a toaster when it produces toast. You know faith is true faith when it produces actions that show we have the love of God in our hearts and that we truly believe in him. Faith is believing in God completely.

Get the Point!

Christian Growth

Object: An unsharpened pencil. You may also wish to have a variety of pencil sharpeners.

Lesson: Building the Christian life takes work.

Text: But continue to grow in the grace and knowledge of our Lord and Savior Jesus Christ (2 Peter 3:18).

Outline

Introduce object: One time I gave new pencils to a group of students from Germany.

1. You sharpen pencils with electric or hand sharpeners or whittling.
2. You sharpen your Christian life with study and prayer, experiences, or failure.
3. A combination of methods is usual.

Conclusion: This pencil will need to be sharpened as I use it and so will you.

One time I gave new pencils to a group of students from Germany. I wondered why they looked at them with such a puzzled look on their faces. Their chaperone told me that the pencils they receive in Germany come with the points already sharpened. They had never seen an unsharpened pencil!

Our pencils most likely come unsharpened because the points can easily be broken in shipment. How do we sharpen them? Using an electric sharpener is the most fun if it doesn't eat up your pencil. Most classrooms have the good old-fashioned sharpeners with the handles. Sometimes you have to use the little sharpeners that you twist. If you are really desperate you can whittle a point with a knife. I have used my fingernail on occasion.

To be a useful Christian, we also need to be "sharpened." One way is to study and pray and learn all that we can about the Christian life. Another is to put our faith into practice and grow and learn from experience as we set about living the Christian life. Some of us charge forth and learn the hard way by bumping into walls, falling down, and having to have God pick us up and head us in the right direction.

Just as we use different ways to sharpen our pencils according to our circumstances, so too we learn about the Christian life in different ways at different times. The more we learn, the more we can avoid the hard way. This pencil will need to be sharpened as I use it, and so will you!

Pick Up God's Silent Signals

Hear His Voice

Object: A TV antenna (or an antenna from a radio or cordless phone).

Lesson: Listen to the still, small voice of God.

Text: After the earthquake there was a fire—but the LORD was not in the fire. And after the fire there was the soft whisper of a voice (1 Kings 19:12).

Outline

Introduce object: This is a TV antenna.

1. It pulls the invisible signal from the air and transmits it to the TV.
2. We have inside antenna to receive the signals of God.
   a. The marvels in nature tell us he is there.
   b. He speaks with a quiet voice inside us.

Conclusion: What else does God say to you?

This is a TV antenna. We used to call it "rabbit ears" because of the way it sticks up. In these days of remote control and cable, you don't see many around anymore. Someday they will be antiques. The purpose of the antenna is to pull the signal out of the air and transmit it to the TV screen. This signal is silent and invisible, but it is certainly there. We can see it on the TV.

We have within ourselves the ability to hear the silent signals that God gives us. It's as though we have an inside antenna if we pay attention to it. Think of the many silent, beautiful things in God's world that tell us he is alive and working: the opening of a flower, the falling of a leaf, a little rabbit hopping through a garden, the warmth of the sun, the glow of the moon, a smile from a friend, a gentle breeze. How great God is!

God also speaks to us deep inside our souls. If you listen carefully, you can hear him. He says, " I love you." What else does God say to *you*?

(Suggestion: Conclude with a period of silence, asking students to think about God and listen for the soft whisper of a voice inside them.)

31

Burning the Candle at Both Ends

Serving Two Masters

Object: A candle—dig out the wick on the bottom so it can be lit from both ends.

Lesson: You cannot serve two masters or try to do too much.

Text: No one can be a slave of two masters; he will hate one and love the other; he will be loyal to one and despise the other (Matt. 6:24).

Outline

Introduce object: Have you heard the expression "burning the candle at both ends"? That's what I'm doing with this candle.

1. When you do this you get used up.
2. You "spill hot wax" (angry words or actions) on those around you.
3. You are restless because you cannot be put down.

Conclusion: You will all need to choose what or whom you will serve.

Have you heard the expression "burning the candle at both ends"? That's what I'm doing with this candle. The saying means that when you do too much, you get used up. You can see that burning the candle this way would use up the candle twice as fast.

There are other things we can learn from this candle. Look at the mess that the candle is making. Hot wax is dripping all over. When you try to do too much (like serve God *and* money; overload your schedule with things you do not need to do; divide your interests in too many ways) you become short of time and temper and drop "hot wax," or angry words or actions, on those around you. That's not good for you, and it is not fair to them.

Another problem with this candle is that I cannot put it down. They don't make candle holders for two-sided candles. If I lay it on a table, the table might catch on fire. If I put it on a metal shelf, it might roll off. It just has to hang here in the air. People who do too much cut themselves off from the normal way of life, from the security of candle holders. They are restless—restless until they can rest in God. To rest this candle, I need to blow out one end and set it in a candle holder. A person must choose activities and interests in life so that one end can be anchored in the security of God's will for them.

You will all need to choose what or whom you will serve.

How to Eat an Orange

Christian Living

Object: A plump, juicy orange

Lesson: Christian living means faith and actions.

Text: But someone will say, "One person has faith, another has actions." My answer is, "Show me how anyone can have faith without actions. I will show you my faith by my actions" (James 2:18).

Outline

Introduce object: How many of you like to eat oranges?

1. You can eat an orange by peeling, cutting, or squeezing.
2. You get to the heart of the Christian life by:
   a. Peeling off outside moodiness, selfishness, and so forth.
   b. Cutting open and removing materialism, love of money, and so forth.
   c. Centering around the will of God and showing faith through actions.

Conclusion: What do you think is the best way of getting to the center of a good Christian life and then sharing it with others?

How many of you like to eat oranges? I always enjoy a nice juicy orange, but getting through the peel can be a challenge.

There are many different ways of eating an orange. Some people peel off the tough skin and split open the juicy sections, eating them one at a time. Other people cut the orange into quarters with a knife and bite off the pulp with their teeth. When I was young, I would cut a round hole in the top of the orange and suck out the juice; then, putting my thumbs into the hole, I would tear open the orange and bite off the pulp. These are all good ways of eating oranges

Getting to the good part of the orange reminds me of getting to the heart of the Christian life. There are things we need to peel off before we can get to the inner, rewarding part. Sometimes on the outside we can appear moody or grouchy. There might be behaviors that make us unattractive to other people. This can be peeled off with God's help. We might need to cut open and remove a streak of materialism, or "I want this and that." Do you have anything in your heart stopping you from living the kind of Christian life God would want you to lead? We can also cut a hole and go right to the heart of the matter by deepening our faith in God, centering ourselves around the will of God for us and then showing our faith through our Christian actions.

What do you think is the best way of getting to the center of a good Christian life and then sharing it with others?

Ouch!

Growing Up

Object: Eye drops (can also use a first-aid solution which stings).

Lesson: Grief and pain are part of spiritual growth.

Text: Happy are those who mourn; God will comfort them! (Matt. 5:4)

Outline

Introduce object: Explain personal use of eye drops.

1. Tears are natural eye drops—crying is healing for grief.
2. Pain is part of learning what is wrong.
3. The pain of lack of confidence is part of growing up.

Conclusion: The best "drops" to help us get through this awkward stage are constant reminders of God's love for us and our worth in his sight.

Whenever I have trouble with my allergies, my eyes get red and swollen. They itch and tear and drive me crazy. The best thing I can do for them is to use these allergy eye drops. When I put them in my eyes they sting for a while but then my eyes start to feel better.

We have natural eye drops to cleanse our eyes. God gave us tears. Tears clean our eyes of dust and other small objects that get into them. Tears are also symbolic of grief—a natural and important way of expressing our emotions of sadness, emotional hurt, or mental anguish. After we cry, we feel better. Thank God he gave us this way of cleansing our souls.

When I put these eye drops in my eyes, it stings. Pain is also important to our growth. We feel pain when we are corrected. We feel pain when we have done something wrong and need to make amends. When we feel pain and discomfort, we know that something is wrong and we strive to change it, just as we feel pain when we touch fire and know to back away from it. We feel pain when we see someone is hurt by what we have said or done, and we know we must do something about it. Pain is important; it helps us grow spiritually.

Pain is also a part of growing up. Sometime between the ages of ten and fourteen, we may feel fat, stupid, and ugly. Just like the ugly duckling, this being uncomfortable with ourselves, struggling to find out who we are and how we fit in, and feeling insecure and self-conscious is a natural part of the pain of growing up. The best "drops" to help us get through this awkward stage are constant reminders of God's love for us and our worth in his sight.